STARTING WITH
CATS

Birgit Gollman

Translated by Astrid Mick
Edited by David Alderton

BLANDFORD

Contents

Introduction

Cats have a very special place among domestic pets. In spite of having attached themselves to human beings thousands of years ago, they have preserved an astonishing independence. They still show many of the behavioural patterns of their wild ancestors and their independence and characters are particularly fascinating. I could never say of any of my cats that it was just like one of its predecessors – even after 20 years of keeping cats.

As a child I used to spend hours playing with our cats. Later, during my school and college years, my tom cat Zorro would keep me company while I was doing my homework and would comfort me with his regular purring. Now that I go out to work, I find my cats sleep or play with each other during my absence and, when I return, they welcome me home and accompany me while I am doing the housework.

I imagine that I shall be keeping cats until I am very old, as I never feel lonely with them in the house. Cats, of all animals, are particularly suitable as pets for people of every age group. The relationship between cats and human beings can be even closer than the relationship between two cats, as some behavioural studies have shown.

My own experiences, which are referred to in this book, are mainly based on keeping ordinary domestic cats of the 'moggy' variety but almost everything said here about these cats also applies to their pedigree cousins.

Things to consider beforehand

It is the almost irresistible charm of small, playful kittens that leads so many people to decide on a cat for a domestic pet. A kitten, however, will rapidly grow up; the charm and novelty wear off, and the daily chores and care associated with keeping a pet can become a nuisance to the owner. The cat may be passed on to someone else, taken to an animal-rescue centre or abandoned. Disease and death are often the result. Therefore, a responsible animal-lover will only decide to have a cat (or any other pet) after careful consideration.

The following ten questions are meant to help you discover whether you would make a good cat-owner. Ideally you should be able to answer 'Yes' to all of them.

- Are all members of your family agreeable to having a cat and are all of them free from any allergy to cats?
- Can you afford to pay for food, veterinarian's bills and other expenses, such as cattery fees?
- Are you prepared to spend a certain amount of time each day, in addition to the regular chores, giving your cat attention (most cats love to have a cuddle with their owners) and to look after it devotedly if it falls sick? If you are away from home a great deal, it would be better not to keep a cat.
- Are you able to cope with the fact that cats will go their own way and will not allow themselves to be trained like dogs, nor allow you to play with them or cuddle them whenever you happen to want to? A cat may readily spit at or bite its owner occasionally if he or she does not respect it's mood!
- Can you cope with cat-hairs on your clothes and carpets, scratch-marks on the furniture, occasional loud miaouwing and cleaning up after your pet if necessary?
- Do you know a place where your cat can be housed safely and looked after while you are away or on holiday?
- Are you aware that cats may live for 15 years or more and that you will be responsible for your cat for a long while, particularly if you obtain it when it is a kitten?
- Is there a quiet spot in your home to which the cat can retreat if it hears loud music or if you are having a noisy party? Cats have very sensitive hearing.
- Have you thought about how a cat will get on with other pets in your home?
- If you live in rented accommodation does your tenancy agreement allow you to keep an animal?

Cats and children

Older cats, because they are more tolerant than younger animals, make ideal companions for children. A cat will put up with a great deal from its human playmates but not with everything. If a child becomes too rough or a game goes on for too long, the cat will either defend itself or walk off. Keeping a cat teaches a child to observe another living creature closely, to have consideration for its moods and to respect its independence. Cats can therefore make a valuable contribution towards a child's education and upbringing.

Occasionally a child will receive a few scratches when playing with the cat – but these will quickly heal and will not harm the relationship. However, be sure to disinfect any injuries and check that children always wash their hands after touching a cat. Slightly older children will also be able to help with looking after the cat and thus will quickly learn to take on responsibility for another creature.

The basic equipment needed for a cat

Some time before your cat arrives, you should purchase all the necessary equipment. A wide range of items is available in pet-stores. The following guidelines may be helpful.

- Glazed ceramic dishes make ideal **food-containers** because they are not easily tipped over and they are also easy to clean. You should provide at least three dishes – for fresh food, dry food and water.
- For a **cat-toilet**, use a plastic tray that is easy to clean. The area of the base should be about 30–45 × 40–50 cm (12 × 18 in), and the sides should be about 10–15 cm (4–6 in) high, lower for a small kitten. Ideally the tray should have a removable top section with incurved edges. This reduces the amount of litter that may be scratched out by the cat. A toilet-house (with a removable top) is particularly useful for cats which are likely to spray urine while standing up or for cats which may be rather nervous. This type of cat-toilet may, however, be rather uncomfortable for large cats! The **cat-litter** should absorb unpleasant odours and should not create any dust. The types of litter that form lumps, making it easier to remove faeces and urine-soaked litter with a **scoop**, are a little more expensive to buy but show savings in everyday use since only part of the lit-ter material need be discarded at a time
- A **carrying container** for transporting the animal is definitely advisable as even a healthy cat will need to be taken to the vet-erinarian regularly. Cardboard carriers, which can be obtained

Opposite: Cats are ideal domestic pets for children. Surprisingly, they will often put up with a great deal from their human playmates but they will also make it quite clear when they have had enough.

A scratching post covered in jute string provides cats with an opportunity to sharpen their claws. The covering can be renewed when necessary.

from a veterinarian or animal-rescue home, and come equipped with ventilation holes and carrying handles, will not prove to be a permanent solution. A **plastic carrier** is better than a cardboard one because it is secure, easy to clean and will not break, even if the cat is sick or urinates during the journey. A **carrying basket** made of willow, which can be opened at the front or the top, has the additional advantage of doubling-up as a sleeping basket, but it can be very difficult to clean thoroughly. Check the attachments and the catch on the door when purchasing a basket. These should be strong enough to resist the attempts at escape of even the strongest cat!

- I cannot recommend buying a **carrying cage** with metal bars; it provides no protection from the elements and gives the cat no feeling of security. Also, when frightened, the animal may try to grab on to you through the bars with its claws.
- A **harness** and **lead** will also prevent a cat from escaping while it is being transported but many cats will scratch and bite if they are unused to travelling and so a secure container will still be needed. A harness offers more security than a collar, which may be ripped off by the cat, whose head is often barely larger than its neck.
- A **scratching post**, covered with sacking or pieces of carpet, will provide a cat with a means of sharpening its claws (which are usually retracted into the pads, so that they will remain sharp). As well as the very simple types that are widely available, you can also obtain, from specialist suppliers, more elaborate **climbing–scratching 'trees'** from specialist suppliers. These are several storeys high and have built-in '**sleeping caves**' and places for **sitting**. The scratching post should be very **stable**. If you want it to be very secure, you can attach it to a wall with brackets. Alternatively you can build your own scratching post – tailor-made for your home – using lengths of wood and left-over carpet. A space-saving version is a simple **plank**, covered in hessian or sacking, that can be fixed vertically to a wall.
- Your cat may not require a special **sleeping basket** as well as a carrying container and, in any case, it will always tend to sleep where it wants to. A hammock-type bed that fits over a radiator often proves popular with cats.
- A **comb** with teeth that are not too sharp and a **brush** with natural bristles are particularly important for grooming the fur of long-haired cats and preventing tangles from developing.
- For cats that are kept indoors all the time a tray of **grass** should always be available so that they can nibble the shoots if they

A tray of grass is important for cats that are kept indoors.

wish. The cat may use the grass to help it vomit up the fur that it constantly swallows when washing itself. This can otherwise collect in its stomach, where a mat, known as a 'fur-ball', may form. Suitable safe grass seed may be bought in garden-centres and pet-stores but you can also plant your own grass seed or wheat grains in shallow trays every 2 – 3 weeks.

- If your cat is allowed out into the garden, it is advisable to install a burglar-proof **cat-flap**. This will enable your cat to go in and out freely as it wishes. Choose a design that is operated by a magnet worn on your cat's collar. This will keep other cats out of your house.
- Windows that are opened regularly should be fitted with **cat-bars** to prevent your cat from escaping or, if you live in a multi-storey apartment block, from plunging to the ground (see 'Is your home suitable for a cat?', see below).
- **Playthings** see 'Cats at play', p. 26.

Is your home suitable for a cat?

How much room does a cat need?
The amount of space that a cat requires is essentially quite small. There should be a corner for the cat-toilet, the best position being in a room with a vinyl or similarly easy-to-clean floor and some facility for ventilation. An area for feeding purposes is also essential. Your cat will be able to get enough exercise, even in a small house, as it is an agile climber and leaper and is not restricted to the floor.

The scratching post can easily be combined with a sleeping den.

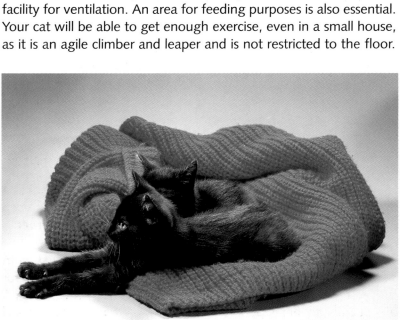

Cats will sleep in a number of different places around the house, the most popular being upholstered furniture, discarded clothes, next to radiators, in cartons, bags, boxes, or sometimes even in the cat-basket ...

Dangers around the house

Just like small children, cats may burn themselves on **hot** irons and hobs, or injure themselves on **sharp** or **pointed** objects (e.g. nails, knives). Tiny objects are occasionally swallowed by cats. **Medicines** and **cleaning agents** may lead to poisoning; keep them in a place that is inaccessible to cats! Some medicines intended for people, such as aspirin, can also be dangerous for cats. Many **indoor plants** (e.g. azaleas, ivy, poinsettias) and cut flowers (e.g. lilies-of-the-valley, carnations) are toxic – do not allow your pet any opportunities to nibble at them! A **plastic bag** left lying about may become a lethal trap for a cat and end in suffocation! Your cat can get trapped in a **door** or **window** that suddenly slams (because of draughts) or is shut violently, or it may get caught in a tilting window. Broken bones or internal injuries may be the result.

A cat-flap will enable cats to get in and out by themselves.

Most cats like to peer out of an open window or observe the outside world from a balcony railing. Your cat may fall off – or even jump out of curiosity! Falls from great heights result in serious injuries or death, even though cats are generally able to land on their feet when they fall. If the animal is uninjured it might then get lost if it is used to living indoors (see 'What to do if your cat runs away', p. 38). As a precautionary measure install **cat-bars** at your windows and do not allow your cat onto an unsecured balcony.

How cats spend their time

Cats are noted for being clean animals but, from time to time, your cat may vomit or mess beside its litter-tray.

Even daily grooming will not prevent **cat-hair** from collecting on upholstered furniture. If this bothers you, try to keep the cat away from the furniture (see 'Can cats be trained?', p. 23) or cover the furniture with a cloth.

Cats love to sharpen their claws on upholstery, textured wallpaper and carpets. Having cats' claws removed by a veterinarian, which is permitted in some countries but not in the UK, is not the answer. This is a cruel practice. The cat will be robbed of the opportunity of climbing or of defending itself in any fight. To avoid **scratch-marks** on your furniture you should attempt to make the scratching post particularly attractive to your cat by

Cat-bars should be fixed to windows that are regularly left open.

A ball – in free fall!

Opposite: Moggies can be obtained without difficulty and, with their short fur, are very easy to care for.

spraying it with an extract of lemon balm or catmint. Most cats love these smells.

Kittens in particular love climbing up **curtains** and this can result in the threads being pulled. The answer is to exclude the kitten from the room or to tie up the curtains out of its reach. In spite of their agility, cats will occasionally knock over objects, e.g. if they are frightened or if they are engaged in a wild game of tag with another cat or with children. China vases, glass figurines and similar ornaments should be kept in a display cabinet for safety.

Where to obtain a cat

You will often hear from **friends** or **acquaintances** about unwanted kittens or stray cats which are in need of a good home. In spring and summer in particular some **pet-stores** offer kittens for sale and these establishments may be able to put you in touch with local breeders. If you have set your heart on a specific breed of cat, you can approach a **breeder** directly. By making enquiries of breed societies or at cat-shows, or by reading the specialist cat-magazines, you should be able to find a breeder near to you. Serious breeders will only part with cats that have a valid vaccination certificate.

A really wide range of animals is offered by **animal-rescue centres**, where you will find cats of all colours, sizes and ages. These poor creatures may have been waiting for a good home for a very long time – and not all of them will be friendly. The small advertisements sections of many newspapers also feature cats and kittens in need of homes.

Choosing a cat

When you are choosing a kitten from a litter it is worth watching the kittens for a while beforehand. Observe them eating, playing and cuddling. Each cat will have its own very distinctive character. Pick a lively, **healthy animal** with bright eyes, a nose that does not run and thick, shiny fur. Staining of the fur below the base of the tail may indicate that the cat has diarrhoea (see 'The sick cat', p. 33–34).

Cats come in a huge variety of **colours** – white, black, red, cream, blue – and in combinations of colours, such as tortoiseshell. Their markings can vary as well, e.g. tabbies may be striped or patched as well as being of different colour combinations. There are no significant character traits associated with colour. One thing that should be remembered, however, is that tortoiseshell cats of any type or breed are almost always female.

A pedigree cat or an ordinary 'moggy'?

Ordinary domestic cats, or 'moggies', that belong to no specific breed, usually have short fur and are therefore relatively easy to care for. They are also not expensive to purchase. You will have to spend quite a bit more on a pedigree cat, depending on its breed and parentage.

Long-haired cats will leave much more hair on carpets, upholstery and clothes than their short-haired relatives and you must be prepared to spend time every day brushing them.

If there is a certain breed of cat that you particularly like, find out about the characteristics of that breed. Persian cats, for example, are known for their tranquil personalities while Siamese cats, on the other hand, can have especially loud and penetrating voices and are athletic by nature.

A kitten or a mature cat?

Kittens should be at least 8 weeks old when they are separated from their mothers, and preferably 12 weeks old in the case of pedigree cats. They are likely to be more playful than fully grown cats and will generally adapt quickly to a new home – but they involve a lot more work! A kitten has to be fed several times a day, it cannot be left alone for long and, to begin with, it will not be house-trained.

A small basket – a wonderful place to take a rest.

If you do not wish to take on the time-consuming task of rearing a small kitten you should choose a fully grown cat.

A male cat or a female?

The sex of a cat will not have much bearing on its character. Both males and females can be quarrelsome, affectionate, moody or lovable. Only in the case of non-neutered, fully grown animals will you clearly notice definite differences in behaviour.

It is quite easy to sex a kitten, even when it is quite young, and you can do this yourself. In a female cat, the genital opening is fairly long and close to the anus. In a male cat, the genital opening is roundish and the distance between it and the anus is noticeably greater than in the female. Before a male cat is castrated, you can also see the paired testicles.

One cat or several?

Most wild cats, and the ancestors of domestic cats are counted among them, are solitary creatures. Even the young will only remain with their mother until they are able to feed themselves. During the course of their evolution into domestic animals, cats have become much more tolerant towards other members of their own species and will often seek contact with them.

You can easily keep two cats in your home. You can leave them alone all day long without having a guilty conscience because they will be able to play with each other. On the other hand, a single cat may become bored and will get up to all sorts of mischief. Some cats will even learn how to open the doors of rooms and other 'containers' – which its owner may well not appreciate. Even the refrigerator, with its understandably alluring contents, may not be safe from a determined and observant cat!

The sides of the dish should not be too high so that little kittens can eat and drink in comfort.

Those of you who are at work all day are recommended to have two cats. Looking after two cats takes hardly any more time, although it does involve more expense. Animals that have grown up together (from the same litter) usually get on well together.

Problems may arise if the second cat is introduced some time after the first and the established cat reacts in an unfriendly manner to the newcomer on its territory (see 'Adjustment period' on p.16.

Adjustment period

In strange surroundings, most cats will feel insecure and be timid to begin with. A young kitten will also suffer from being separated from its mother and siblings. Do not expect your kitten to want to cuddle and play with you right away because it will need time to get used to you.

If you have a large house or apartment, it is a good idea to confine the cat to just one quiet room with places to hide and 'look-out' points (to which you should be able to gain access as well). During the first few days, you should put the cat's litter-tray or box in this room and feed the cat there. The following advice is intended to help ease your cat's adjustment to a new environment and to gain its trust.

- To begin with only one family member should be present in the room with the cat.
- Avoid hasty movements and loud noises near your cat.
- Speak quietly and in a friendly manner to your cat but do not stare at it – direct eye-contact is off-putting.
- Do not try to take the cat or kitten out of its carrying container or from a hiding place, try to stroke it against its will or pick it up. Rather, wait patiently until it comes to you of its own accord or seeks contact with you.
- Many cats can be coaxed with titbits – or, if they are in a playful mood, with a movable object (e.g. a ball of paper tied to a piece of string).
- How long it will take your cat or kitten to adjust depends on its character as well as on its previous experiences. Young kittens usually quickly accept their new owners as substitute mothers or siblings. This was the case with my cat Bunyip.

Cats from animal-rescue homes may have had bad experiences in the past and often take a very long time to lose their mistrust of people. Have a lot of patience with these animals. Our tom cat Menelaos, a stray, hid from us for a whole week and refused to eat but, after 10 days, he was already purring at us from a safe distance. Now he is a completely tame lap-cat.

Small balls are ideal toys for cats, who will play with them for hours on end.

Friendships between cats

Young cats that are obtained at the same time, or within short intervals of each other, usually accept each other quite quickly and get on together for the rest of their lives.

A fully grown animal that has never had to share its home with another cat will often react in an unfriendly manner towards a

16

strange cat in its territory. Many adult cats will even be afraid of young kittens! Please consider that you may be spoiling an older cat's last years if you introduce its successor during its lifetime.

An established cat will obviously be at a certain advantage on its own territory and will have the upper hand over a newcomer, as long as the stranger does not happen to be considerably larger, stronger or cheekier. Give the new cat time to adjust to one room on its own before you allow the two cats into contact with each other.

Try not to interfere during their first encounter. As long as both cats have ample opportunity to escape or find a hiding place there should be no serious injuries. Nevertheless, in case you do have to intervene, keep a pair of leather gloves handy.

Please do not neglect your first cat in favour of the second (it will become quite jealous, and rightly so) but give each of them its fair share of stroking.

Nevertheless, it occasionally happens that two cats never really make friends with one another. If your house is too small and the two cannot get out of each other's way and are continually brawling, it might be best to look for a new home for the second cat.

Should your cat be allowed outdoors?

Exploring outdoors comes fairly close to the natural lifestyle of a cat and offers more variety than life inside the house. Cats that are allowed to go outdoors do not need to use the litter-tray so often and they are also able to sharpen their claws on real trees. Thus they will save their owners a lot of work – and probably the cost of a scratching post as well!

With patience, cats and dogs can be taught to get used to each other. Occasionally they will even become genuine friends.

Outdoor cats, however, lead a more dangerous life than those that are kept permanently indoors and, on average, do not live as long. Many cats die prematurely on our roads every year and they are also likely to encounter diseases when roaming outdoors.

Every cat-owner will have to decide for his- or herself whether to subject a cat to the risks of a free life. Personally I would only recommend allowing your cat outside if you have a garden which has a high fence and is not situated beside a busy road. Your cat should also really feel at home in your house and must be allowed to get used to you before you open the door to the garden – or it might run away.

Cats are so agile and mobile that they almost always manage to turn as they fall and so land on their feet.

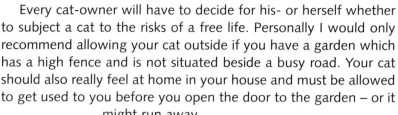

Other risks of a free-roaming life

Many cats (particularly fearless ones) become victims of vehicles, either directly, as a result of **traffic accidents**, or indirectly, by drinking **antifreeze**, which is deadly for them.

For most cats **poisoning** through eating rat-poison or poisoned rodents will usually prove fatal.

Frequent causes of **injuries** are barbed-wire fences, broken glass and fights with other cats, dogs or other animals.

Your cat may accidentally become **shut in** a tool-shed or garage.

To prevent a cat being classed as a stray, and being **caught** and taken to an animal-rescue home (pedigree cats are often stolen), it can be **tattooed** in its ear when young or fitted with an elasticated collar, complete with a disc or capsule giving the owner's address and telephone number.

Another option is to have a coded microchip implanted beneath its skin (as simple as a vaccination). The code number of the cat can then be entered in a register for a small fee and the owner can be traced quite rapidly by this method. Many veterinarians and animal-rescue centres have the scanners necessary to read the code of the microchip.

18

The right foods for your cat

Cats have a typically carnivorous pattern of dentition. The long, sharp canine teeth, which are ideal for holding onto prey, coupled with the pointed incisors, which enable it to tear up its prey, are both indications that cats are first and foremost predatory in their feeding habits.

Their natural prey consists of mice and other small rodents, which are eaten whole (skin, bone and all, usually even with the contents of their stomach and intestines). These prey animals contain all the vital proteins and smaller amounts of energy-laden fats and carbohydrates, roughage, and important minerals and vitamins. Cats will also take in minerals and vitamins by eating grass. They get most of their liquid requirements from their food but will also drink water.

A harness with a lead will prevent a cat from escaping when outside the house. Only very few cats like being taken for walks on a lead and training should begin at an early age.

Types of cat-foods

Substitute foods given to a domestic cat should contain all the vital nutrients in properly balanced proportions. The use of ready-prepared food is recommended for owners who are out at work all day. If you have more time you can prepare your pet's food yourself.

This kitten is looking suspiciously at the milk in this dish and is using its paw to 'test' it.

Dry food may be too hard for young cats and, at this stage, is regarded as more of a plaything.

Three-quarters of **home-prepared foods** should consist of **lean meat** of different types. This should be cooked so that your pet will not acquire any diseases or parasites from its food. For a change, you can offer your cat **fish**, removing the bones first. **Offal** should **not** be given regularly because it does not provide a balanced diet. Moreover, the Vitamin A contained in liver may cause irreversible damage to the cat's joints.

Suitable **additional foods** are cooked oats, potatoes or rice, all of which will provide the necessary carbohydrates. Grated fruits or vegetables, e.g. carrots – lightly cooked, will fulfil any extra vitamin and roughage requirements. You can occasionally add a little cooked egg to the food. If you are using ready-prepared foods, supplementary vitamin and mineral preparations are usually recommended only for growing kittens and pregnant females but they can be beneficial if you are relying just on fresh foods of the type described above. Discuss their usage with your veterinarian because overdosing can be as harmful as a deficiency in some instances.

Any change-over from one type of food to another, e.g. from canned to fresh food, should be carried out gradually over the course of a week or so, to minimize the risk of digestive upsets. Avoid relying on just one type of food as this could easily lead to deficiency symptoms in your cat. Never give your cat food directly from the refrigerator; warm it up slightly first.

Gnawing at **bones** is good for your cat's teeth as it prevents the formation of plaque. Do not, however, give your cat any poultry bones as they can easily split and pieces may become wedged between its teeth or could injure the cat's digestive tract if swallowed.

Nowadays **canned foods** contain all the necessary nutrients in the correct proportions and they can be used on their own. A wide

Opposite: A fish makes a welcome change of diet.

Here are three firmly based dishes, one each for fresh and dry food and another for drinking water.

choice of ready-prepared foods will guarantee a varied menu for your cat. You can also obtain special foods for kittens and older cats.

Dry foods, while incorporating all the necessary nutrients, contain very little water. Many cats tend not to drink enough to compensate for this lack of liquid, even if there is a bowl of water right beside their food-container. As a result, manufacturers of such foods have added salt to increase the cat's thirst. Because of this, you must make sure that your cat has access to fresh drinking water. Dry foods have the advantage of being less likely to attract flies or to go off in hot weather, as well as helping to keep the cat's teeth clean.

Every kind of sweet food is **completely unsuitable** for cats, and so are fatty, highly spiced scraps of food from the table. Remember that, in comparison with human beings, cats require less carbohydrate but more protein in their diet.

How much food will your cat need?

The amount of food that your cat will need depends on its age, size and its activity level. Growing, pregnant or nursing cats have a particularly high food requirement.

Proceed according to your cat's appetite. If you can see your cat getting fatter, however, you should cut down on its daily food ration. Problems are most likely to arise if your pet has been neutered.

Where, when and how should you feed your cat?

Cats are creatures of habit. For this reason, feed your cat at the same times and in the same (quiet) place. Of course, each cat should have its own food-container, which should be washed after every meal.

Newly weaned, 8-week-old kittens should be fed at regular intervals six times a day. On successive months you can leave out one meal until, from the sixth month, they will manage on two meals a day (e.g. in the morning and evening). Fully grown cats can even have their entire rations once a day although often not all of the food is eaten right away and it dries out or, at worst, attracts flies. Therefore only offer an amount which is likely to be eaten within a few minutes.

Dry foods can generally be left available throughout the day, provided that they do not become wet.

Regular grooming of the fur is necessary, particularly in long-haired cats. A brush with natural bristles and a comb with teeth that are not too sharp will help.

The right drinks for your cat

A bowl of **water** should always be placed near the food-dish and the water should be changed daily.

Milk is not a thirst-quenching drink but a food. Because of the high amount of lactose (milk sugar) which it contains, it may cause diarrhoea in some cats (even if it is diluted), particularly Siamese cats, which lack the enzyme to digest this substance. You may offer your cat a specially formulated feline milk, sold in cartons in pet-stores, which contains only insignificant amounts of lactose and so should not produce any harmful side-effects.

Care and bathing

A cat-owner's daily chores consist mainly of **feeding** the cat and **cleaning out the litter-tray** and replacing the soiled litter. The litter-tray should also be disinfected and washed out thoroughly with hot water at least once a week.

Cats spend a great deal of time washing themselves. They should be **brushed** frequently, especially in the spring, when they are moulting their thick winter coat, so that they do not end up swallowing too much hair or rubbing it off against the furniture. In the case of long-haired cats, this should be done on a daily basis, otherwise the fur will become matted.

You should only ever **bathe** a cat if its fur is very dirty. Use handwarm water and a cat- or baby-shampoo. After its bath, rub the cat with an old towel and keep it in a warm room, free of draughts, until it is quite dry. Many cats resent being bathed, so it may be advisable to wear a pair of gardening gloves, to guard against being scratched or bitten.

Dirty ears can be cleaned with a cotton-wool bud dipped in olive oil. The task will be easier if a helper can hold the cat firmly. Do not push the bud down into the ear.

Occasionally it will be necessary to clean your cat's **ears** with a piece of cottonwool dipped in olive oil. Cats kept in pairs often clean out each other's ears, thus saving their owner a lot of trouble.

If your cat's **claws** are too long, you can use special scissors, available in pet-stores, to cut off the excess part that does not contain any blood vessels. Should you be in any doubt, ask your veterinarian for advice because, if the claws are cut too short, they will bleed.

Can cats be trained?

Cats have a definite will of their own and are only partly prepared to be subordinate to their human owners. They vary greatly in this

respect, from very unusual individuals that follow their owner like a dog to those that are almost completely untrainable. Usually, you will find that compromises are reached between the cat and its owner. The success of any attempts at training will depend to a degree on the character of the individual cat, as well as on the patience and persistence of the owner.

For example, if you want furniture without **scratch-marks**, every time your cat tries to sharpen its claws on the sofa you will have to shoo it off or carry it to its scratching post. Never hit your cat if it does something it has been forbidden to do, or it may become afraid of your hand. It is a far better idea to startle the cat with an unpleasant sound, or to spray it with a little water. Some cats will also learn to respond to the command 'No', spoken in a sharp voice. Spend a lot of time with your cherished pet – bored cats are much more likely to get into mischief.

Avoid allowing your cat to form habits that could become a nuisance, e.g. begging at table. It can be quite difficult to get rid of such habits once they have become established.

Many cats will learn to come running if they are called, particularly if they know that a meal is waiting for them.

Get your cat used to a harness and lead when it is young if you wish to exercise your cat safely in an area close to a road. For most cats, a collar and lead are sheer torture.

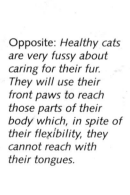

A small scoop made of plastic helps remove lumps of faeces and urine-soaked cat-litter from the litter-tray (above).

Opposite: Healthy cats are very fussy about caring for their fur. They will use their front paws to reach those parts of their body which, in spite of their flexibility, they cannot reach with their tongues.

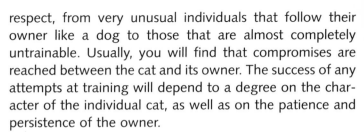

House-training your cat

Cats are naturally clean animals and, outdoors, will bury their faeces and urine. Indoors, it will usually be sufficient to show them their litter-tray.

Your cat may occasionally decide to leave its mess somewhere else for any of the following reasons:

- The litter-tray is already soiled. Empty the tray more often or provide a second one.
- The cat is suffering from diarrhoea and was unable to get to the litter-tray in time.
- Female cats in season and male cats sometimes spray urine as an encouragement to other cats. Neutering should help.
- Some cats, by their dirty habits, are protesting against being shut in or against another cat being given preferential treatment.
- Your cat happens to be one of the rare specimens that will never be clean.

Always make sure to clean the spot which has been soiled thoroughly or your cat might use it again. (Cleaning agents containing ammonia are unsuitable as they contain similar substances to cat's urine and the smell will serve to attract the cat back to the spot!) There is absolutely no point in pushing the cat's nose into its mess. Instead, carry your cat to the (clean) litter-tray whenever it becomes restless and starts carrying out scraping motions with its front paws. It will soon get the idea and this will help in most cases.

Cats and people as partners

In contrast to popular opinion cats are not bonded just to their homes. They are well able to distinguish between acquaintances and strangers and will recognize good friends after years. They will often develop a preference for one member of the family – and this need not always be the one who feeds them. Solitary house-cats in particular need the affection and company of their adopted human. Their needs will depend on the age and idiosyncrasies of the animal: young

cats need to be played with; older cats especially need companionship.

Stroking and picking up your cat

Cats show their affection in many different ways: they will rub against your legs, hold out their head, allow themselves to be lifted onto your lap while purring loudly, or follow your every step. Most cats love to be stroked – but only when they are in the mood.

When responding to your cat, always consider its mood and which type of affectionate behaviour it prefers. If it feels neglected it will attract your attention with loud miaouwing.

Cats at play

Kittens practise their innate hunting skills by playing with their siblings or with inanimate objects, lurking, stalking, leaping and hitting out with their paws. Cats kept in pairs are able to keep each other occupied but, in the case of solitary animals (particularly house-cats of any age), you will have to make time for playing with them every day. In this way you will keep your pet young and fit and prevent boredom.

All kinds of toys for cats – rubber and fur mice, balls, etc. – are available from pet-stores and similar outlets. Even an ordinary table-tennis ball (perhaps hidden in a box with holes) or a ball of paper dragged on a piece of string will keep a cat entertained for hours. It is important that you make sure that your cat cannot hurt itself on the toy or swallow any part of it.

Balls of wool are dangerous for a cat: it can become tangled up in the wool or its legs may become tied up and its circulation cut off. The fibrous wool may get caught on the cat's tongue and may be partly swallowed, causing the cat to choke.

Cats particularly like to be scratched in places that they cannot reach with their tongues. You can even feel the purring if you pass your finger over their throats.

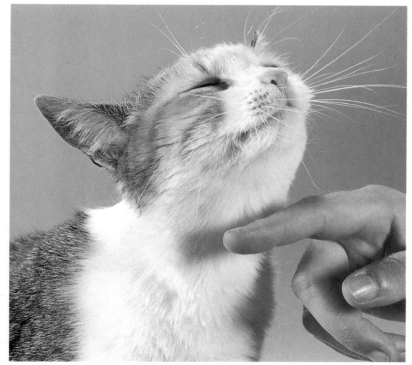

Opposite above: *The right way to carry a cat: support the back legs with one hand and hold the animal with the other, with your arm giving support to the front legs.*

Opposite below: *A cat offering its head for stroking. This is a trusting cat greeting a human friend.*

27

Fabric or fur mice are likely to be popular toys.

Getting to know and understand your cat

To really understand your cat you have to be able to think yourself into its position. This is not quite easy as cats see the world in a very different way from human beings.

A cat's ears, just like its tail, provide a good indicator of its mood.

Senses

A special light-reflecting layer (the *tapetum lucidum*) in a cat's **eyes** enables them to 'shine' when a ray of light falls on them in the dark. This layer enables a cat to see efficiently in faint light and cats can certainly see far better than we can at night. However, even a cat cannot see anything in total darkness.

A cat's mobile **ears** will be able to pick up even very faint noises and extremely high-pitched sounds (in the ultra-sound range) that would be inaudible to human ears. Its highly developed sense of touch – the whiskers are particularly sensitive – enable the cat to find its way around in the dark.

The **nose** of a cat is far more sensitive to smell than the human nose. Cats have scent glands on their chins, lips and foreheads, with which they leave a scent mark – undetectable to us – when they rub themselves against us. Their territory is marked with urine and gland secretions.

In bright light a cat's pupils will form vertical slits whereas in darkness they become large and round.

Vocalizations

The **miaouwing** of a cat can express many things – hunger, a plea to be stroked or have a door opened – but it can also be a mating call. If you listen carefully, you will soon be able to distinguish the different calls.

Purring shows that the cat is feeling good and is often accompanied by 'treading' with the paws. The claws on the front paws are alternately pushed out and withdrawn while a cat does this (as a kitten your cat stimulated the milk-flow from its mother in this way).

Hissing, **spitting** and **growling** mean that the cat is afraid but ready to defend itself. If a cat is attacked it may screech loudly. A swelling and subsiding **yowling** and miaouwing, often accompanied by **deep growling**, can be heard when two rival males are fighting. One very peculiar sound is a kind of **'quacking'**, in which the jaws are opened and closed as if in a cramp. This is made when interesting prey – e.g. a bird – is near but still out of the cat's reach.

Body language

An observant person can gauge the mood of a cat by its facial expression, body posture and the position of its tail.

As regards **facial expression**, a friendly attentive cat has its ears pointed upwards and forwards. A threatening cat will turn its ears to the side while a defensive cat will place its ears and whiskers flat against the sides of its head.

The **posture of the tail** in a friendly cat greeting its owner will be erect and vertical. Twitching of the tip is a sign of intense concentration, while violent movements of the tail indicate restlessness, bordering on annoyance in certain situations.

A cat will often wash itself as a gesture of embarrassment, e.g. if it is not sure about something, or if its owner has discovered it doing something which it knows is forbidden.

Opposite: Indistinguishable – alert and attentive?

Two examples of a cat's body language. Left: In a friendly cat the ears are pricked and usually pointing forwards. Right: The slightly turned-back ears and lifted paw show that the cat is nervous but ready to defend itself.

The sick cat

A healthy cat has bright clear eyes, a moist but not runny nose, clean ears, thick, shiny fur, clean teeth and pink gums. Its faeces will be firm and dark and its urine clear and yellow. The animal will be lively and have a good appetite.

Symptoms of illness

If your cat's **eyes** are cloudy, weeping or secreting pus, this may indicate an injury, a foreign body in the eye or an infection. If the third eyelid partly covers the eye this may indicate an eye problem or general bad health; it is often linked with weight loss.

A brown discharge from the **ears**, combined with itching (indicated by scratching) suggests ear mites or an infection, often with a combination of bacteria and fungi. If your cat holds its head to one side and often shakes it, there may be a small foreign body, such as a grass seed, stuck in its ear. Never try to locate the object by poking anything into your cat's ear as this could cause injury. Only a veterinarian can help in this instance.

Tri-coloured 'lucky' tortoiseshell-and-white cats like this one are almost always female.

A runny **nose** or frequent sneezing can indicate a whole range of infectious diseases.

Bad breath is often linked to problems with teeth and gums. The cat will try not to chew, or chew only on one side. The veterinarian will be able to treat the affected teeth under an anaesthetic and remove any plaque. Diseases of the gums can also be caused by viral infections.

If your cat **coughs**, with a stretched-out neck, it is often merely trying to bring up fur-balls. If it also produces a lot of **saliva**, it may have something stuck in its throat.

Gasping breath may be due to excitement but may also be caused by an infection of the respiratory system, such as bronchitis, asthma or pneumonia. In the case of pneumonia, your cat would also have a temperature.

Vomiting may have harmless causes: your cat may have eaten too much or is bringing up a fur-ball. If it continues, and your cat appears ill and depressed, the cause could be more serious, such as poisoning or an infectious disease.

Diarrhoea can be caused by the wrong diet (e.g. milk). Allow your cat to fast for 24 hours; it should be allowed only to drink black tea or an electrolyte solution. After that give it small portions of cooked rice and white meat. In the case of a kitten, however, seek veterinary advice because it can dehydrate very

rapidly. Should the diarrhoea persist, or if there is blood in the faeces, this may indicate an infectious disease or possibly a severe infestation with worms (see 'Parasites', p. 35).

There is cause for alarm if your cat is apathetic, has no appetite, will not drink or is trying in vain to urinate. Do not try to treat the cat yourself and never give it medicines intended for human beings, but take it to the veterinarian as quickly as possible. Remember: sick cats require a lot of quiet, warmth and loving care.

Wounds and broken bones

The **small wounds** that cats sustain in fights will usually heal by themselves. If there is a lot of **bleeding**, however, it may be necessary to apply a pressure bandage. If bleeding persists seek veterinary advice as suturing may be necessary in the case of a bad wound. Bite wounds will often develop into **abscesses** that swell up and then exude pus or there may be an inflammation of the subcutaneous tissue that will require treatment by a veterinarian.

If you have just become a cat-owner you should find out the address of your nearest veterinary surgery so that you can contact it immediately should there be a need.

In cases of **broken bones**, often caused by falling from a great height or getting a paw squashed in a door, only a veterinarian will be able to help.

Keep calm when handling an injured cat, talk to it and keep it warm. This will help to lessen the shock resulting from the accident. Be careful – when in a state of shock a cat may bite even its beloved owner.

Infectious diseases and vaccinations

Where infectious diseases are concerned, for cats, just as for people, preventive care is better than treatment. Viral illnesses cannot be treated with antibiotics and so vaccination is used to give protection. All vaccinations will be entered onto the cat's vaccination record by your veterinarian.

Kittens can be vaccinated for the first time at the age of 2 months against **cat influenza** (a febrile inflammation of the respiratory tract that often leaves lasting damage) and **feline infectious enteritis**, or panleukopenia (a usually fatal viral infection involving the digestive system); a second vaccination will be necessary 3–4 weeks later. These vaccinations will need to be repeated every year.

Two vaccinations, at the ages of 9 and 12 weeks respectively, are necessary to protect your cat against **cat leukemia**. Afterwards a booster shot once a year will be sufficient.

In areas where **rabies** occurs, free-ranging cats should be vaccinated at the age of 3 months; this will have to be repeated annually. The UK and Australia are currently free of rabies so cats are not vaccinated against this killer disease in these countries. Elsewhere, including parts of the USA, vaccination may be compulsory.

One of the latest developments in this field is a vaccine to protect against **feline infective peritonitis** (FIP), although this may not yet be available in all countries. Two vaccinations, at the ages of 16 and 19–20 weeks respectively, provide good protection against this illness. Subsequently an annual vaccination will be sufficient to maintain the level of immunity needed to safeguard your cat's health.

Parasites

Cats that are allowed to go outdoors are likely to be repeatedly infested with **fleas** and **ticks**, and possibly also **mites** and **lice**. These parasites can transmit various diseases.

A flea-collar impregnated with insecticide will help to protect your cat from these pests. The collar should have a safety-break – a small section made of elastic so the animal can free itself if it gets caught up in bushes. If your cat suffers an allergic reaction (reddened skin) to the insecticide, or if you have several cats that wash each other, you may wish to use one of the new products which prevent fleas from feeding. In some cases, these can be given

with your cat's food. Always read and follow the instructions carefully when using such products. Otherwise the health of your cat could be adversely affected. As part of controlling fleas, the places where the cat sleeps or sits must be cleaned and disinfected as flea eggs and larvae can survive for months in cracks in the floor or under carpets.

Any ticks that have attached themselves to your cat should be dabbed with a piece of cottonwool dipped in petroleum jelly; this will make them fall off. A helper should hold onto the cat while you are doing this.

The most common internal parasites in cats are **roundworms** and **tapeworms**. Cats that are allowed outdoors, especially those which eat mice or are heavily parasitized by fleas, should be wormed every 3–6 months, with a preparation prescribed by the veterinarian, to combat tapeworms. Roundworms can also be spread directly from mother to kittens and, again, regular treatment is essential for their well-being.

This plastic carrier comes with a detachable lid, which makes it easier to lift out the cat.

Illnesses which can be spread to people

- **Rabies** is an infectious disease that may also be fatal to human beings (see also 'Infectious diseases and vaccinations', p. 35.)
- **Toxoplasmosis** is caused by single-celled organisms (protozoans), which can be identified in the faeces of cats. The disease is particularly dangerous to unborn human babies. It is important for pregnant women to wear gloves when emptying a cat-litter-tray and be particularly careful about hygiene when handling their cats. Usually, however, infection in human beings occurs by eating infected meat that has not been cooked properly.
- **Roundworm** eggs may be ingested by young children, e.g. when sucking their thumbs. The larvae can then, very occasionally, cause severe illness (*toxocariasis*) if they reach susceptible organs (the brain and eyes).
- **Ringworm** is a fungal skin infection that may cause damage to the hair – in round patches – and itching in human beings. It is characterized by circular red patches on the forearms. Transmission can be prevented by speedy treatment of the cat by a veterinarian, as well as thorough regular cleaning of the cat's accessories.

This carrier is the best type for a trip to the veterinarian.

Taking your cat to the veterinarian

Even a healthy cat should be taken to the veterinarian once a year for its annual vaccinations. Try to keep the stress levels to which the cat will be subjected during transport and in the surgery as low as possible by preparing well for the visit:

- Arrange an appointment at the veterinary surgery and arrive a few minutes beforehand, although sometimes, if an emergency crops up, the appointment may run late.
- Line the carrying container with a cloth; in the case of a basket place a piece of plastic sheeting under the cloth.
- Do not feed your cat just before setting off because it may be sick on the way.
- Some cats are afraid of the carrier and will hide away when they see it. Shut the cat in a room where it has no places to hide before getting out the carrier.
- If your cat is reluctant to be placed in the carrier and sticks out its legs so that you cannot get it through the opening, or claws itself onto you, try wrapping it in a cloth so that its legs are held against its body. You will find that it fits into the basket quite easily; and will disentangle itself from the cloth without difficulty in due course. Waste no time in getting it to the veterinarian. Protect the cat from draughts and inclement weather during the journey.

A responsible cat-owner will use the services of a veterinarian when the condition of a cat deteriorates and it can no longer live without suffering pain.

The old cat

Cats live for about 15 years on average but some have lived for more than 20 years. The record is held by a cat in England which lived to the age of 35 years.

From the beginning of the second decade of it's life a cat will become quieter and less active. Very often symptoms of old age – similar to those in human beings – appear, e.g. a reduced capacity to see and hear and signs of damage to the joints.

If your cat has problems with its teeth it should be given only finely chopped food and, if necessary, this should be presented as several small portions a day, because an older animal's appetite may decrease.

Be considerate of your cat's problems and give it a peaceful old age. If you notice that your cat is in great pain, hard as it may be, let it be put to sleep to save it from unnecessary suffering. Your veterinarian will always be able to advise you. For older cats, regular health checks every 6 months or so are recommended.

This hunchbacked posture shows clearly that this cat is ready to attack. The fur is raised and bristling, making the animal appear as large as possible.

No kitten could resist a hiding place like this.

What to do if your cat runs away

If you allow your cat to go outdoors, sooner or later you will find that it does not return at the usual time. In most cases it will have found a second home where, for some reason, it has stayed longer than usual but it may have had an accident, been locked up somewhere or even been hit by a vehicle. You should not wait too long before setting out to look for it. If a genuine house-cat escapes you should immediately try to find it and catch it again as such animals are not generally able to cope with the dangers present outside. The following measures will help you to find your cherished pet again:

- Hunt around your own property or the surroundings of your house thoroughly, calling your cat's name as you do so. Take some food with you!
- Ask your neighbours to check whether your cat is in their garden or shut up somewhere.
- Put up notices in suitable places, e.g. bus-stops, shop windows, with an exact description and a photograph of your cat. Do not forget to include your telephone number.
- Inquire regularly at all relevant animal-rescue centres, catteries, lost-property places and the police station to determine whether your cat has been found. Asking all the veterinarians in the neighbourhood is also worthwhile, in case your cat has been found injured.
- You could even place an advertisement in the local newspaper.

It is important not to give up too soon – your cat may return safe and sound even weeks later!

Care during your holidays

During a brief absence (1–2 days) a programmable feeding device will ensure that your cat receives its food at the usual times, although you must ask a friend or neighbour to check on your pet, and to provide it with fresh water every day.

In the case of long holidays you can choose from the following options: you can take the cat with you, which is usually impractical; have someone look after it at home; give it to friends; or place it in a cattery.

Holidays with your cat

Most cats only feel at ease in familiar surroundings. During long car or train journeys cats suffer from being shut in carrying containers and from the noise. Often they will find it impossible to eat, drink or use the litter-tray. You should really only take your cat with you if you regularly spend time in the same holiday spot, e.g. a weekend home, or if your cat is devoted to you and would find it hard to cope with a lengthy separation. It is often not possible to take cats abroad because of health regulations.

Care at home

In my opinion the best solution is to ask a neighbour or a friend to look after your cat, which means feeding it, emptying its litter-tray, and spending some time with it every day.

The cat should know the person looking after it. In some areas there are cat-sitter clubs whose members will look after cats either for a fee or on an exchange basis.

How will your cat get on with other domestic pets?

Cats and **dogs** are not, as you might suppose, always sworn enemies. They can be persuaded to get used to each other, in spite of the initial language difficulties. If they grow up together they may even become good friends. On the other hand, if the dog is introduced to the household after the cat you should on no account allow the cat to feel that it has taken a back seat. It might feel put out and become very jealous.

Small rodents, **rabbits** and **birds** may be attacked by cats, as prey, if they are allowed to run about or fly freely. I recommend keeping them all in cat-proof cages. A cat which has never been given animal prey (dead or alive) by its mother does not know that it can eat mice but it will instinctively chase after any small animal that runs away from it.

Some cats learn to distinguish between huntable prey and animals that belong to the family. My cat Schnurrli never touched our guinea-pig, although she had access to the outside run. However, when our neighbour's guinea-pigs escaped, they were chased and killed by several cats, including Schnurrli, over a period of several days. Therefore do not take the risk and keep your cat away from any other pets which could be potential prey.

Aquariums should have a cat-proof cover or your cat may decide on a little fishing – or even take an unintentional bath!

A bird fluttering about will awaken the hunting urge in a cat. A wise cat may learn that its feathered house-mates, kept in cages or aviaries, are not to be regarded as prey – but never take the chance of leaving them together!

Breeding

It is fascinating to watch a litter of kittens growing up but finding good homes for them is very difficult. Far too many cats end up unwanted in an animal-rescue centre or have to be put to sleep. Sensible cat-owners will therefore have their cats neutered at about 6 months of age, unless they are sure of finding good homes for the kittens. Pedigree kittens, particularly those with a good parentage, are usually easier to place. However the stud fees for a recognized pedigree male cat can be quite high.

Opposite: *Sometimes kittens will see human fingers as playthings which they can nibble.*

Facts and figures

Gestation period	About 9 weeks
Litters per year	2–3
Kittens per litter	3–6 (1–8)
Birth weight	90–140 g (3–5 oz)
Eyes first open	After 7–12 days
Solid food from	3–4 weeks
Weaned	6–8 weeks
Ready for new home	8–12 weeks

Pregnancy

About 4 or 5 weeks after mating, the pregnant cat's belly will start to appear visibly rounded and her teats will become enlarged. She will gradually become quieter and will avoid high leaps and strenuous climbing.

Towards the end of her pregnancy she will require a little more food, divided into several smaller meals. Make particularly sure

Below left: *This female cat is demonstrating her readiness to mate and offering herself to a male cat by hollowing her back and making short, tripping steps with her back paws.*

Below right: *A female cat in season will roll about on the ground, often howling loudly if she thinks a male cat is nearby.*

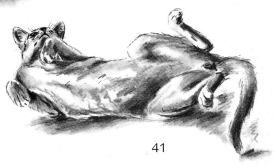

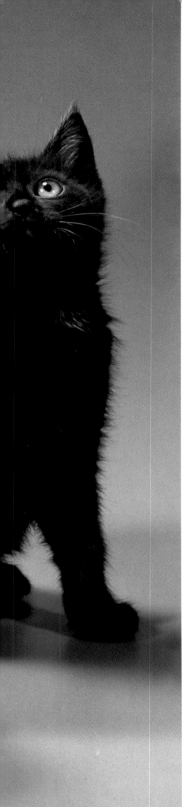

that she is receiving enough protein, minerals (especially calcium) and vitamins.

The birth

The cat will look for a quiet, secluded place to give birth; this should be warm, dry and draught-free. A few days before the birth stop her from going outside as she might choose an inaccessible hiding place in which to give birth to her kittens. Prepare an upholstered box or basket for her. A thick layer of newspaper will serve to soak up the waters and the blood, and a clean cloth should be spread over them. Both the cloth and the newspapers should be removed after the birth.

The birth will generally be easy, with no problems. The kittens will be born at intervals of about 15 minutes to several hours. Stay close by but on no account disturb the cat. Only if the birth does not seem to be progressing after a long period of time may your cat need help, preferably from a veterinarian. It is extremely rare for an inexperienced or very nervous mother cat to eat her own young.

The new-born kittens will still be blind and their sparse fur will be wet and sticky with birth tissues. They will immediately be cleaned by their mother, who will bite through the umbilical cord. Instinctively the tiny kittens will search for the teats and begin to suckle. Usually the female will eat only some of the afterbirth; the remainder should be removed.

Opposite: Curious little kittens watch everything that moves.

Cats have an average of three to six kittens. Litters of eight or ten kittens sometimes occur.

Rearing the kittens

A nursing cat requires large quantities of food, in balanced proportions, divided into three to four meals. To begin with the mother cat will spend nearly all her time with her kittens, suckling them, washing them and keeping them warm. Many cats do not like it at all if anyone touches the kittens or takes them out of their nest. Even the most placid of cats can become quite aggressive if she believes her kittens are being threatened.

Frequent disturbances may lead the mother cat to change the nest. She will carry each kitten by the scruff of its neck while the kitten adopts a still carrying pose. At 2–3 weeks of age the kittens will begin to explore their surroundings, at first by crawling. As soon as the kittens are eating solid food they should be offered a litter-tray (the sides should not be too high).

Pedigree cats

In cats, as in other domestic pets, mutations (genetic alterations) have occurred during the course of time which have produced different colour variations and types of fur. These features have only been bred for systematically, for about 100 years.

Pedigree cats must conform to a particular **standard** that describes certain characteristics, such as length of fur, shape of face and body, and colour, which have been laid down by the various **breed associations.** According to type of fur, cats are often divided into long-haired, semi-long-haired and short-haired breeds.

The breed associations regularly organize **exhibitions** at which the best animals of each breed receive awards.

Long-haired cats

A flattish face, a stocky body and relatively short legs are typical of **Persian Long-hairs**. There is a range of recognized colour variants. The **Colour-pointed Long-hair**, also called the **Himalayan** in

Left: *The Maine Coon from North America belongs to the group of semi-long-haired cats. Cats with this type of fur will still need grooming every day.*

Below: *The short, smooth, shiny fur is typical of Burmese cats.*

North America, is marked in a similar way to a Siamese cat and is considered to be a separate breed, although it resembles the Persian Long-hair in terms of appearance and 'type'.

Semi-long-haired cats

The fur of these cats is also quite long but the shape of the head is distinctly different from that of the Persians. They include: the **Norwegian Forest** cat; the very similar **Maine Coon**; the **Birman**, which has dark patches of fur on its ears, head, tail and legs, but otherwise has light-coloured fur and white paws; the **Turkish Van** cats, which have auburn or cream patches on their faces, and a similarly coloured tail, but are otherwise white; and the **Somali**, which has bands of light and dark ticking on the individual hairs. Semi-long-hairs tend to have longer coats in the winter than during the summer.

Short-haired cats

Well-known breeds include: the **European** and **British Short-hairs**, which look rather like the ordinary moggy, although they are larger; the **blue-grey**, or **Chartreux**; the slender, blue-eyed **Siamese**; the slightly stockier, often brown **Burmese**; the **Abyssinian**, which is the short-coated form of the Somali cat; the **Oriental** cats, which are bred in a wide range of colours; the **Rex** cats, whose fur is curly or wavy; and the often tail-less **Manx** cat.

Siamese cats are known for their blue eyes and loud voices.

Index

Picture sources
Colour photographs are by Regina Kuhn, of Stuttgart. Black-and-white illustrations are by Siegfried Lokau, of Bochum.

Acknowledgements
My thanks go to all those whose tolerance and help allowed me to keep cats for so many years: my mother, my husband and special thanks to my grandmother. Comments by veterinarians Alice Kelner and Georg Gassner helped improve the manuscript. BG

A BLANDFORD BOOK
First published in the UK 1997 by Blandford
A Cassell imprint
Cassell plc
Wellington House 125 Strand London WC2R 0BB

Text copyright © 1997 Cassell plc
Translated by Astrid Mick
Originally published as *Katzen* by Birgit Gollmann
World copyright © Eugen Ulmer GmbH & Co.,Stuttgart, Germany

Distributed in the United States by Sterling Publishing Co., Inc., 387 Park Avenue South, New York, NY 10016-8810

A Cataloguing-in-Publication Data entry for this title is available from the British Library

ISBN 0-7137-2682-2

Printed and bound in Spain